Where does our food come from?

pany

com

Created by Bobbie Kalman

Author and Editor-in-Chief
Bobbie Kalman

Educational consultants
Elaine Hurst
Joan King
Jennifer King

Notes for adults
Jennifer King

Editors
Kathy Middleton
Crystal Sikkens

Design
Bobbie Kalman
Katherine Berti

Photo research
Bobbie Kalman

Print and production coordinator
Katherine Berti

Prepress technician
Katherine Berti

Illustrations
Katherine Berti: page 9

Photographs
Comstock: pages 3 (milk), 12 (top), 18 (milk
    and butter)
Photodisc: page 21 (top right)
Other photographs by Shutterstock

Library and Archives Canada Cataloguing in Publication

Kalman, Bobbie, 1947-
    Where does our food come from? / Bobbie Kalman.

(My world)
Includes index.
Issued also in electronic format.
ISBN 978-0-7787-9565-0 (bound).--ISBN 978-0-7787-9590-2 (pbk.)

    1. Food--Juvenile literature. 2. Nutrition--Juvenile literature.
I. Title. II. Series: My world (St. Catharines, Ont.)

TX355.K3435 2011   j641.3   C2010-907446-7

Library of Congress Cataloging-in-Publication Data

Kalman, Bobbie.
 Where does our food come from? / Bobbie Kalman.
    p. cm. -- (My world)
 Includes index.
 ISBN 978-0-7787-9590-2 (pbk. : alk. paper) -- ISBN 978-0-7787-9565-0
(reinforced library binding : alk. paper) -- ISBN 978-1-4271-9672-9
(electronic (pdf)
 1. Food industry and trade--Juvenile literature. I. Title.

 TP370.3.K35 2011
 641--dc22
                                                    2010047128

Crabtree Publishing Company
www.crabtreebooks.com   1-800-387-7650

Printed in China/022011/RG20101116

Published in Canada
Crabtree Publishing
616 Welland Ave.
St. Catharines, Ontario
L2M 5V6

Published in the United States
Crabtree Publishing
PMB 59051
350 Fifth Avenue, 59th Floor
New York, New York 10118

Published in the United Kingdom
Crabtree Publishing
Maritime House
Basin Road North, Hove
BN41 1WR

Published in Australia
Crabtree Publishing
386 Mt. Alexander Rd.
Ascot Vale (Melbourne)
VIC 3032

What is in this book?

What do you eat?

Most people eat different kinds of foods.

What foods do you eat?

What foods do you not eat?

Where do foods come from?

foods made
from grains

milk, cheese,
eggs, meat

other
foods

fruits and vegetables

Grain foods

Foods made from **grains** are foods we eat every day. Bread, cereal, and pasta are all made from grains.

pizza crust

cereal

pasta

Breads and cereals are made
from wheat, corn, oats, and rice.
We eat corn and rice, too,
just the way they are.

wheat bread

corn on
the cob

bowl of rice

Growing grains

Grains are the seeds of grasses.
Grain plants grow in huge fields,
like the ones shown on these pages.

wheat field

wheat grains

Whole grains contain every part of the grain. They are the healthiest grains for us to eat.

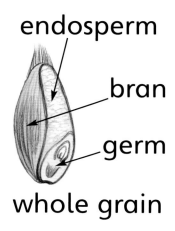
endosperm
bran
germ
whole grain

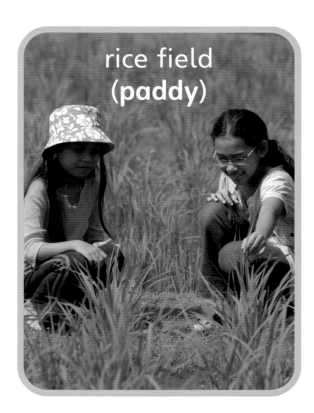
rice field
(**paddy**)

corn field

9

Vegetables are great!

Vegetables are great for us!
Lettuce, cabbages, beets, and
carrots are some vegetables.
Which are your favorite vegetables?

Ask your parents if you can grow a vegetable garden. You will love the fresh-tasting foods!

Fabulous fruits

Fruits also contain many things that our bodies need.

Many fruits taste sweet.

Strawberries taste sweet.

Strawberries grow in fields.

Apples and some other fruits grow on trees. Bananas and oranges also grow on trees. They grow in places that are hot all year long.

apple tree

Bananas grow in hot places.

Help from bees

Did you know that much of the food we eat needs help from bees? Bees make plants healthier so they can make a lot of food.

14

Bees fly from flower to flower to collect **nectar** and **pollen**. Pollen is a yellow powder plants need to make fruit. Bees take pollen from one plant to another.

nectar

pollen

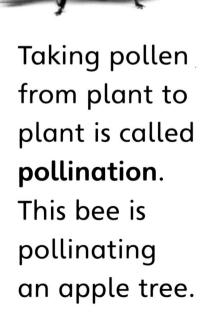

Taking pollen from plant to plant is called **pollination**. This bee is pollinating an apple tree.

15

Sweet plants

Bees help plants grow, and they also make **honey**. They make honey from the nectar in flowers. Honey is sweet and yummy!

Another sweet liquid that comes from plants is **maple syrup**. Maple syrup is made from the sweet **sap** of maple trees.

Maple sap drips out of a maple tree into a pail. The sap is then boiled until it becomes syrup. Maple syrup tastes great on pancakes!

maple → tree

pail

17

Foods from animals

Meat, milk, cheese, and eggs are foods that come from animals.

cheese

milk

butter

cow

goat

Cheese and butter are made from milk.
Cows and goats give milk.

Eggs come from chickens.

Eggs are a great breakfast food!

Healthy choices

Some foods are healthier than other foods. Here are some healthy food choices for you.

yogurt

whole-grain pasta and bread

fruits of
all kinds

fresh vegetables
grown in your garden

beans of all kinds

21

Did you know?

Some vegetables are fruits. Fruits grow from flowers, and they contain seeds. Tomatoes, peppers, and cucumbers are just some of the fruits we eat as vegetables. Which other "veggies" have seeds?

seed.

Words to know and Index

animal foods
pages 5, 18–19

cheese

eggs   milk

fruits pages
5, 12–13, 15
21, 22

grains
pages 5, 6,
7, 8–9, 20

honey
page 16

maple syrup
page 17

pollination
pages 14–15

vegetables
pages 5,
10–11, 21, 22

Notes for adults

Objectives
- to have children identify the foods they eat
- to teach children about food groups
- to have children learn where different foods come from
- to encourage children to identify healthy food choices

Before reading
Ask the children:
"What foods do you eat for breakfast?" (also lunch, dinner, snacks)
"What foods don't you eat?" (possibly meat, dairy, peanuts, junk food)
Look at the title page and ask the children:
"Where did the girl get the bread from?"
"What is the bread made from?"
Show some different grains to the children. Have them guess which grains they are and what might be made from each grain. Show grain products such as oatmeal or noodles and ask them to match the grains and products.

Questions after reading the book
"What are the three kinds of fields where grains grow in the book?" (rice, wheat, corn)
"List a food you eat made from the grain in each field." (rice, cereal, corn, pasta, bread)

"Name three vegetables you like to eat."
"Where does fruit grow?"(trees, plants, fields)
"What do bees do to help plants?"
(Explain why pollination is important.)
"What products come from animals?"
(cheese, milk, yogurt, butter, eggs, meat)
"What are some healthy foods?" (home-grown vegetables, beans, fruits)
"Why is it important to eat healthy foods?"

Activities: Pie graph
Give children a pie graph with four food groups labeled: grains, animal products, fruits and vegetables, and other. Then have children draw the foods they eat under each heading.
Describe a type of food and have the children guess what it is and where it belongs. Example: I am long and green. Sometimes I am in a salad.
Answer: celery (vegetable)
Make bingo cards with a variety of foods and food groups. Play Food Group bingo.

Extension:
Discuss the food shortage that many children around the world face.
Plan a toy or bake sale to raise money for an organization that helps feed hungry children.

For teacher's guide, go to www.crabtreebooks.com/teachersguides